JUMPSTARTING
JavaScript

BUILD A TWITTER BOT AND LED ALERT SYSTEM WITH NODE.JS AND RASPBERRY PI

Lynn Beighley

Maker Media, Inc.
San Francisco

Published by
Maker Media, Inc.
1700 Montgomery Street, Suite 240
San Francisco, CA 94111

Maker Media books may be purchased for educational, business, or sales promotional use. Online editions are also available for most titles (safari-booksonline.com). For more information, contact our corporate/institutional sales department: 800-998-9938 or corporate@oreilly.com.

Publisher: Roger Stewart
Editor: Patrick DiJusto
Copy Editor: Elizabeth Welch, Happenstance Type-O-Rama
Proofreader: Scout Festa, Happenstance Type-O-Rama
Interior Designer and Compositor: Maureen Forys, Happenstance Type-O-Rama
Cover Designer: Maureen Forys, Happenstance Type-O-Rama

December 2017: First Edition

Revision History for the First Edition

2017-12-13 First Release

See oreilly.com/catalog/errata.csp?isbn=9781680454970 for release details.

978-1-68045-497-0

Safari® Books Online

Safari Books Online is an on-demand digital library that delivers expert content in both book and video form from the world's leading authors in technology and business. Technology professionals, software developers, web designers, and business and creative professionals use Safari Books Online as their primary resource for research, problem solving, learning, and certification training. Safari Books Online offers a range of plans and pricing for enterprise, government, education, and individuals. Members have access to thousands of books, training videos, and prepublication manuscripts in one fully searchable database from publishers like O'Reilly Media, Prentice Hall Professional, Addison-Wesley Professional, Microsoft Press, Sams, Que, Peachpit Press, Focal Press, Cisco Press, John Wiley & Sons, Syngress, Morgan Kaufmann, IBM Redbooks, Packt, Adobe Press, FT Press, Apress, Manning, New Riders, McGraw-Hill, Jones & Bartlett, Course Technology, and hundreds more. For more information about Safari Books Online, please visit us online.

How to Contact Us

Please address comments and questions to the publisher:

Maker Media, Inc.
1700 Montgomery Street, Suite 240
San Francisco, CA 94111

You can send comments and questions to us by email at
books@makermedia.com.

Maker Media unites, inspires, informs, and entertains a growing community of resourceful people who undertake amazing projects in their backyards, basements, and garages. Maker Media celebrates your right to tweak, hack, and bend any Technology to your will. The Maker Media audience continues to be a growing culture and community that believes in bettering ourselves, our environment, our educational system—our entire world. This is much more than an audience, it's a worldwide movement that Maker Media is leading. We call it the Maker Movement.

To learn more about Make: visit us at *makezine.com.* You can learn more about the company at the following websites:

Maker Media: *makermedia.com*
Maker Faire: *makerfaire.com*
Maker Shed: *makershed.com*
Maker Share: *makershare.com*

CONTENTS

PREFACE: WHAT IS NODE.JS?

JavaScript is a programming language that web browsers can run. Browsers like Firefox and Chrome are built with *engines* that can understand and execute programs written in the JavaScript language. Firefox has an engine called SpiderMonkey, and Chrome's engine is called V8.

Running JavaScript in a browser limits what you can do with it. For example, with JavaScript in a browser, you are limited to interacting with web pages. You can detect errors when people enter information in a form. You can open browser windows and alert boxes. But you can't control anything outside of a browser.

Fortunately, you have another option. When you install and use the JavaScript extension Node.js, your JavaScript code can run independently of a web browser. (You'll often see Node.js simply called *Node*, and that's what we'll do for the rest of this book.)

Node is the V8 JavaScript engine bundled together with libraries that handle input/output and networking. This means that Node lets you use JavaScript outside of a browser to run shell scripts, manage back-end services, and run directly on devices.

What You Bring to the Book

* Basic familiarity with programming concepts

* Ability to set up and connect a Raspberry Pi

* Ability to access and use a console

* Understanding of sudo, directories, and file creation/editing

1

Meet JavaScript and Node.js!

This chapter takes you through the steps to install Node on your Mac, Windows, or Linux OS. Then you'll check to see that it's working.

> NOTE As you install Node, you may notice that something called *npm* is also being installed. This program is the Node Package Manager.
>
> Node is really popular, and it has a whole new ecosystem of useful Node-based code packages other developers have created for you to use. When you want to use one of these packages in Node, you need an easy way to install and manage them. That's what npm does for you—it installs additional Node packages you want to use.

Follow the instructions for your system; then jump to the last section, "Node Is Installed; Now What?"

INSTALL NODE ON MAC

Although you could build Node from the source code, this guide is all about getting you going quickly. The easy way is to visit the official Node website, Nodejs.org, and use an automated installer. Here are the steps involved:

Step 1. Visit *nodejs.org/en/download/* and click the Macintosh Installer button to download the installer (Figure 1.1).

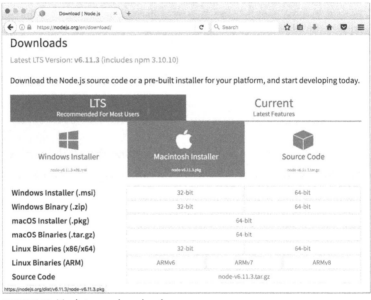

FIGURE 1.1: Nodejs.org download page

Step 2. Find the file you downloaded and double-click it. You'll see the installation dialog (Figure 1.2). Click Continue to go through the installation. Stick with the default settings.

Step 3. When the installation finishes, you'll see a summary screen with installation information (Figure 1.3).

FIGURE 1.2: Node installer

FIGURE 1.3: Node installer summary

Step 4. You need to make sure that /usr/local/bin is in your PATH environment variable. To do this, open the Terminal.app

program—you can find it under /Applications/Utilities. Start
the Terminal program. In the new terminal window, type

```
echo $PATH
```

This will return a list of directory paths, separated by colons.
In my case, I get this output:

```
/usr/local/bin:/usr/bin:/bin:/usr/sbin:/sbin
```

You can see that /usr/local/bin is the first thing in my
PATH. If you don't see it in yours, you'll need to add it. If you
do see it, skip step 5.

Step 5. Here's how to add /user/local/bin to your PATH. In
your terminal, type

```
touch ~/.bash_profile
```

This creates the file if it doesn't already exist. Now type

```
open ~/.bash_profile
```

This opens the .bash_profile file in TextEdit. In TextEdit, add
the line

```
PATH=${PATH}:/usr/local/bin
```

Save the .bash_profile file and quit TextEdit.

You'll need the changes you made to take effect. To do this,
type this command in the terminal:

```
source ~/.bash_profile
```

Step 6. Let's confirm that we have Node running. Type this
command in your terminal to see the versions you've installed:

```
node --version
```

You'll see output like this, giving you the version of Node that you just installed:

```
v6.11.3
```

Don't worry if the version number is different from what you see here; new releases come out frequently.

After confirming you have the Node program installed and working, you're ready to start writing JavaScript. Leave this terminal open and skip ahead to the section "Node Is Installed; Now What?"

INSTALL NODE ON WINDOWS

You'll start by visiting the official Node website, Nodejs.org, and getting the automated installer. Here are the steps involved:

Step 1. Visit *https://nodejs.org/en/download/* and click the Windows Installer button to download the installer (Figure 1.4). Pick the MSI file for either 32 bits or 64 bits, depending on your computer platform.

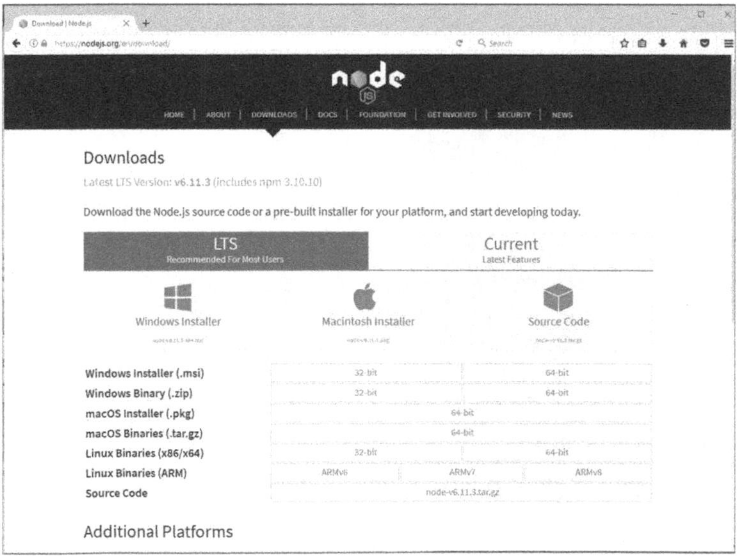

FIGURE 1.4: Nodejs.org download page

Step 2. Find the file you downloaded and double-click it. You may get a warning dialog asking for permission to install. Click OK.

The installation program opens (Figure 1.5). Click Continue to go through the installation. Stick with the default settings.

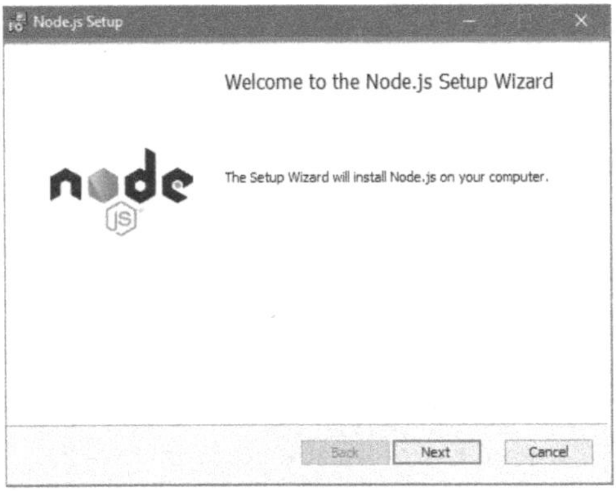

FIGURE 1.5: Node Setup Wizard

Step 3. When the installation finishes, you'll see a summary screen with installation information. Let's confirm that we have Node running. Click your Start menu, and you should see two new menu items under Recently Added: Node.js and Node.js Command Prompt (Figure 1.6).

FIGURE 1.6: Windows Start menu

Step 4. Click Node.js Command Prompt to open the prompt. You'll see a terminal window open with this line:

```
Your environment has been set up for using Node.js 6.11.3 (x64)
and npm
```

Don't worry if the version number is different from what you see here; new releases come out frequently.

This confirms that you have the Node program installed and working. You now have everything you need to start writing JavaScript. Leave this terminal open and skip ahead to the section "Node Is Installed; Now What?"

INSTALL NODE ON LINUX

The easiest way to get going with Linux is to install a prebuilt binary package from the Nodejs.org website.

> **NOTE** If you're an experienced Linux user, you may find it simplest to use the package manager for your particular Linux distro. You can find a rundown of those at *nodejs.org/en/ download/package-manager*.

Step 1. Visit *https://nodejs.org/en/download/*. Download the 32- or 64-bit file with a name like `node-v6.11.3-linux-x64.tar.xz` where `v6.11.3` is the current version (Figure 1.7). Be sure to save it in a directory you'll remember. I'm saving mine to my `Downloads` directory.

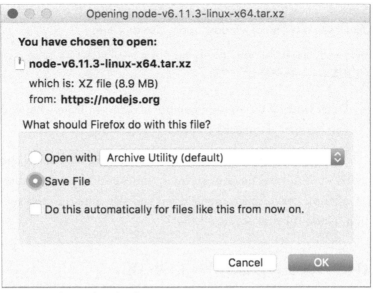

FIGURE 1.7: Linux download

Step 2. This archive contains everything you'll need and is organized into subdirectories. You can extract it where it needs to go by using these commands:

```
~$ cd ~/bin
~$ tar xz ~/Downloads/node-v6.11.3-linux-x64.tar.xz
```

> **NOTE** If ~/bin does not exist, you'll need to create it first.

Step 3. Make sure you have your PATH set to find your Node installation. Edit your .bash_profile file and include that line. You can do so with this command:

```
~$ PATH=$PATH:~/bin/node-v6.11.3-linux
```

or by editing your `.bash_profile` and adding this line:

```
PATH=${PATH}:/usr/local/bin/node-v6.11.3-linux
```

Step 4. Use this command to check to see whether Node has been installed:

```
node --version
```

and you should get output with the version number

```
v6.11.3
```

Don't worry if the version number is different from what you see here; new releases come out frequently.

This confirms that you have the Node program installed and working. You have everything you need to start writing JavaScript. Leave this terminal open and continue to the next section.

NODE IS INSTALLED; NOW WHAT?

At this point, you should have Node installed and a terminal or console window open. (From here on, we'll just call it the terminal.)

In the next chapter, you'll write your first program, but let's quickly try out the Node REPL.

> **NOTE** The REPL is like a playground where you can try out JavaScript code. It's installed along with Node. REPL stands for Read Eval Print Loop. The REPL gives you a quick and easy way to test your JavaScript code and fix any mistakes.

In your terminal, type **node** to start the Node REPL:

```
$ node
```

Notice that your cursor has changed to a greater than sign (>).
You're now interacting with the REPL. Let's output some text:

```
> console.log('Hello World!');
Hello World!
undefined
```

If you're getting an error of some kind, check your punctuation. Make sure you've got single quotes around the text and a semicolon at the very end of your code.

Did You Get Back *undefined*?

Don't worry if you did! You're using a JavaScript function, which will **always** return undefined if it doesn't have a return value (you'll learn more about this later). For now, you can just ignore it. You haven't made any mistakes.

Now try this very handy .help command:

```
> .help
.break Sometimes you get stuck, this gets you out
.clear Alias for .break
.exit  Exit the repl
.help  Show repl options
.load  Load JS from a file into the REPL session
.save Save all evaluated commands in this REPL session to a file
```

NOTE Commands starting with a period are talking to the REPL interface—they're not JavaScript code.

And let's close the REPL and get back to the regular command prompt, using the `.exit` command:

```
> .exit
```

You've installed Node, and you know how to start up and quit the REPL. This means that you're ready to learn some JavaScript. Chapter 2 awaits.

2

Getting into JavaScript

Y ou played with the REPL at the end of the last chapter. Now you'll begin learning JavaScript by writing code both in the REPL and into saved JavaScript files.

STRINGS, MATH, AND THE REPL

You've already used the REPL (also called the Node shell). If it isn't open, go ahead and launch it. In Windows, open a command prompt or click the Node.js Command Prompt that you installed in your Start menu. On Mac or Linux, open a terminal.

Type **node** to start the REPL. Remember, you're in the shell when the prompt changes to >.

The REPL is handy as you learn JavaScript. You can test pieces of your JavaScript code before saving them to a file. When you make an error in the REPL, you'll get immediate feedback.

Let's try making a deliberate mistake so you can see the feedback you get from the REPL.

Try this broken line of code:

```
> console.log(It's broken)
```

Although there are several things wrong with this code, you'll get only one message at a time. Here's the first error:

```
console.log(It's broken);
            ^^^^^^^^^^
SyntaxError: Invalid or unexpected token
```

Let's fix the first problem. If you look at the carets under the text It's broken, you'll see they start right under the single quote.

In JavaScript, anytime you use a string of text, you need to put it in quotes. Otherwise, the REPL thinks those words are code. So now try this:

```
> console.log('It's broken');
```

Argh! You get a hanging ellipsis.

```
console.log('It's broken');
...
```

This time the REPL finds the beginning of the string, but it thinks the second quote is closing your text. It's looking for a parenthesis to end the command.

This is tricky. We want to use a quote in our string, but we need quotes around our string. The simple way to fix it is to use double quotes around the whole string so you can use the single quote in the string.

Both single and double quotes can be used around strings of text:

```
> console.log("It's broken");
It's broken
undefined
```

(Remember, you can ignore the undefined!)

You can put more than a single string of text in the parentheses of the console.log function. Try these commands:

```
> console.log('Hello'+'world');
```

This command combines the two strings and outputs the single string Helloworld. If you want a space between the two words, you can use any of these three arguments in the parentheses; they'll all work.

```
'Hello '+'world'
'Hello'+' world'
'Hello'+' '+'world'
```

You won't always be using strings, though—you'll be using lots of numbers and variables. Here's a quick look at some of your options; try them out.

```
> console.log(42);
> console.log(5 + 4);
> console.log(5 * 4);
```

Numbers don't use quotes; the REPL recognizes them. And you can do math operations on them.

FUNCTIONS

You've used your first built-in function, `console.log`. This simple function prints out whatever string or other value you put in parentheses.

Now let's write a function! A *function* is basically code that can be reused. There's more to it than that, but you'll start with something simple. Try typing in the following function. (Don't type the ellipsis; it indicates that the REPL is waiting for more code that you can enter on the next line. Press Enter/Return and use multiple lines.)

```
> function countPets(){
var dogs = 2; var cats = 1;
var total = dogs + cats; return (total);
... }
```

Here's what is going on in this function:

```
function countPets(){
```

This line starts with the JavaScript keyword `function` so the REPL knows a function is coming.

`countPets()` is the name of the function. Everything in the function goes inside curly braces.

Next are two lines beginning with the JavaScript keyword `var`. It's short for variable, and the lines are saying that the variable `dogs` is equal to 2 and the variable `cats` is equal to 1.

The next line says that the variable `total` contains the sum of `dogs` and `cats`.

The keyword `return` instructs the function to send back the value of `total` after the function finishes.

To use the function, type this command:

```
> countPets();
```

You'll get back the sum of `dogs` and `cats`: 3.

Let's make the function a little more reusable. Take a look at this code and see if you can guess what's going on.

```
> function countPets(dogs, cats){
... var total = dogs + cats;
... return (total);
... }
```

Now try it!

```
> countPets(5, 3);
```

In this function, you're passing in values that the function can use. Being able to add different values to the same code is part of what makes functions so useful!

You've now had a taste of JavaScript code. Unfortunately, as soon as you end this REPL session, your functions will not be saved. It's time to move out of the REPL and put your code into .js files so you can start simple and build on them.

USING JAVASCRIPT FILES

The REPL is great for testing, but you need to be able to save and reuse your code. You'll need a text editor so you can write and edit your JavaScript code and save it into a file.

Start by creating a text file called **fromfile.js**. Put this code in your file and save it to a location you'll remember:

```
console.log('These words are from my .js file!');
```

In your terminal, navigate to the same directory where your fromfile.js was saved and type this command on your command line (not in the REPL!):

```
$ node fromfile.js
```

Node will execute the code in your file and you'll see the output on your screen.

MAKE A WEB SERVER

Now that you can save .js files, you can start exploring the real power of Node. Without Node, you can write JavaScript code that would run only on an existing web server. But Node frees you from those browsers and lets you create your own web server!

It's easy to create a little web server with Node. Begin by creating a file called **easyserver.js** and save this code in it:

```
var http = require('http');
var server = http.createServer(function(req, res) {
  res.writeHead('I created this server!');
  res.end();
}
);
server.listen(8080);
```

Now try running your server. I'll explain this code after you try it. In your terminal, visit the command line in the directory where you saved the file. Type

```
$ node easyserver.js
```

The terminal will seem to hang, but that's fine—it means your server is running!

Open a browser and visit the URL localhost:8080. You should see the line I created this server! (Figure 2.1).

I created this server!

FIGURE 2.1: A web page with output from your web server

After you visit the web page, press Ctrl-C in your terminal to end the program.

Let's take a closer look at what's going on in this code. I don't expect you to understand it right now. I've added comments to the original code. Just try to get the gist of it!

```
var http = require('http');
var server = http.createServer(function(req, res) {
  //send response to client
  res.writeHead('I created this server!');
  // finish the response
  res.end();
});
//the web server is listening on port 8080
server.listen(8080);
```

Node is doing most of the work for you with built-in code. The very first line is calling the http module, which, behind the scenes, has the code to turn your running program into a web server. The require keyword is giving the new variable http access to a whole lot of saved Node code and functions that can create a web server.

In the second line, the code is calling a function called createServer. Whenever anyone connects to your web server, the code in that function will be executed.

The last line tells the server you created to start listening for incoming requests on a particular port (in this case, 8080).

Comments in Your Code

The double slashes you saw in the last code example let you add comments to your code. Node ignores any words following the //. Comments are great for helping you remember what you did in your code.

In the next chapter, you'll begin using JavaScript to build a Twitter bot!

3

Creating a Node Twitter Bot on Raspberry Pi

You've written your first JavaScript program. Next, you'll learn how to create a Twitter bot with Node that can run on any machine that has Node installed, including your Raspberry Pi.

By now, you should already have Node installed on your system. This chapter will take you through the steps you need to set up and authorize a Twitter account, connect that account to a JavaScript program, and use the `twit` `nmp` module in your program to do most of the work.

CREATE AND AUTHORIZE YOUR TWITTER ACCOUNT

If you don't have a Twitter account for your bot, create one at Twitter.com.

Do You Use Gmail?

Twitter accounts are based off unique email addresses. If you don't have a spare email address but you use Gmail, you can save the hassle of creating a new email address with a handy trick. Gmail lets you add a plus sign and a few letters to your address.

For example, if your Gmail address is jane-doe@gmail.com, you can create other email addresses like janedoe+twitterbot@gmail.com or janedoe+catbot@gmail.com.

Twitter will think this is a new address, but Gmail will place everything sent to that address into your existing inbox.

One interesting side effect: It's relatively easy to set up a Gmail filter to label all messages sent to that address as "Twitterbot Email" or something similar. That way, you can see at a glance which emails have been sent to your bot.

Step 1. Log into the Twitter account you'll be using for your bot.

Step 2. Visit *apps.twitter.com* and click the Create New App button.

Step 3. You'll be presented with a form to fill out (Figure 3.1). Complete all the fields. You can enter any website you wish, and make sure you type a URL in the callback field. Don't worry too much about what you enter in the fields now; you can change the contents at any time.

Step 4. Click the Developer Agreement check box and click Create Your Twitter Application.

Step 5. You'll now see a summary page. Click the Keys And Access Tokens tab (Figure 3.2). The keys on this page connect your Twitter app to the Node bot program you'll create later in this chapter.

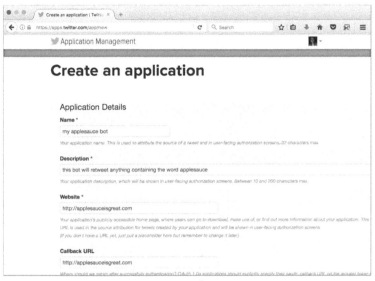

FIGURE 3.1: Creating a new Twitter app form

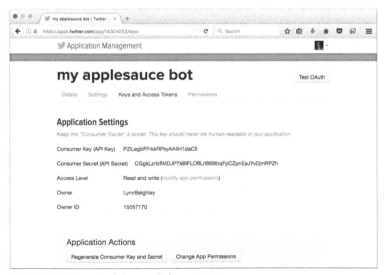

FIGURE 3.2: Keys And Access Tokens page

Step 6. Scroll to the bottom of this page and click the Create My Access Token button. This page now displays an access token and access token secret (Figure 3.3). Leave this page open. Next up, you'll create a file in your terminal and copy and paste info from this page into it.

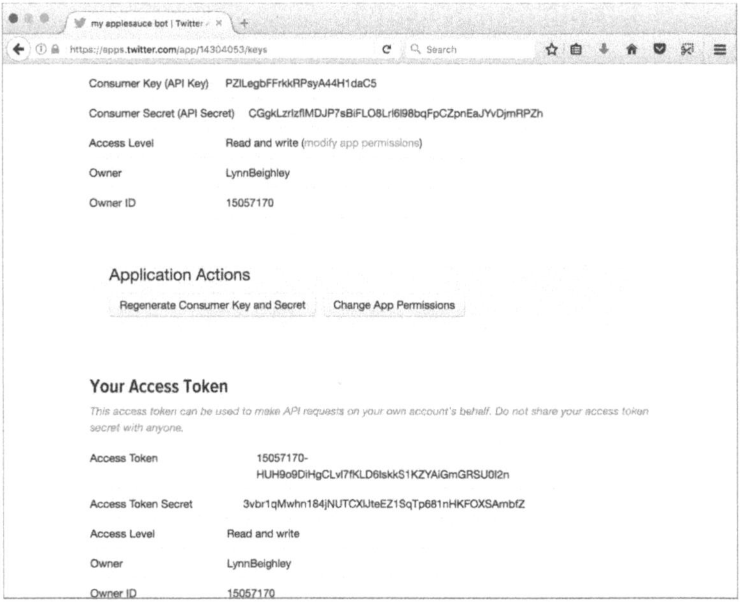

FIGURE 3.3: Keys for your Twitter application

In the next section, you'll set up a directory, initialize it, and create a configuration file with the keys and tokens on this page.

CREATE A CONFIGURATION FILE

Open your terminal on the device where you installed Node.

Create a new directory where you can keep all your new Twitter bot files. I'll call mine newtwitbot. Navigate to your new directory:

```
pi@raspberrypi:~ $ mkdir newtwitbot
pi@raspberrypi:~ $ cd newtwitbot
pi@raspberrypi:~/newtwitbot $
```

Our Twitter bot will use two files: `config.js` and `index.js`. Create them now with the `touch` command:

```
pi@raspberrypi:~/newtwitbot $ touch
config.js index.js
pi@raspberrypi:~/newtwitbot $ ls
config.js index.js
```

We need to edit the `config.js` file with the Twitter keys for your app. Using the editor of your choice (I use nano), edit your `config.js` file as shown here. Substitute your keys in place of the *xxxxx* values:

```
//config.js
/* TWITTER APP CONFIGURATION
   consumer_key
   consumer_secret
   access_token
   access_token_secret
 */
module.exports = {
  consumer_key: 'xxxxx',
  consumer_secret: 'xxxxx',
  access_token: 'xxxxx',
  access_token_secret: 'xxxxx'
}
```

Now, the Twitter bot's configuration is complete. These four values will be unique for each Twitter application you create.

CREATE THE TWITTER BOT

Do you remember the npm application you installed along with Node? This handy application lets you reuse code other people have previously written.

There's already a Twitter code library called `twit`. We can import this library with npm and then use functions to make communication with Twitter much easier.

To install this library, use this command:

```
pi@raspberrypi:~/newtwitbot $ npm install --save twit
```

You'll see this output:

```
npm notice created a lockfile as package-lock.json. You should
commit this file.
npm WARN newtwitbot@0.0.0 No description
npm WARN newtwitbot@0.0.0 No repository field.
+ twit@2.2.9
added 55 packages, removed 55 packages and updated 1 package in
15.243s
```

After the twit package has finished installing, open the index.js file. We'll start adding lines. (Don't worry about the WARN lines! If we were building code to then store for other people to use, we would want to add a description. In this case, we aren't.)

Building the *index.js* File

If you get lost, don't worry. The complete contents of the index.js **file are listed at the end of this chapter.**

Open index.js in an editor and add these lines. They tell our bot to use the twit code and let the code access the Twitter application keys in the config.js file.

```
// Dependencies
var twit = require('twit'), config = require('./config');
```

Now under those lines, add the following:

```
var Twitter = new twit(config);
```

This line creates a variable called Twitter, a special object that has access to all the code in the twit library, as well as the keys we set up in the config.js file so that it can actually communicate with Twitter. (This is confusing, but think of this Twitter variable as a superhero. It's more than just a single value; it can access lots of custom functions built to do things with Twitter like post, retweet, and favorite. This will be clearer by the end of the chapter.)

Next we'll get to the heart of our bot. We'll start by making it find tweets that contain the text strings doggo or pupper. Then it will use the console.log function you've already seen and post any found tweets to your terminal.

Add this function, called retweet, to your index.js file:

```
var retweet = function() {
  var params = {
    q: 'doggo OR pupper',
    result_type: 'recent'
  }
  Twitter.get('search/tweets', params, function(err, data) {
    // if there no errors
    if (!err) {
      // grab ID of tweet to retweet
      var retweetId = data.statuses[0].id_str;
      // Tell Twitter to retweet
      Twitter.post('statuses/retweet/:id',
      {
        id: retweetId
      },
      function(err, response) {
        if (response) {
          console.log('Retweeted!!!');
        }
        // if there was an error while tweeting
        if (err) {
          console.log('Error tweeting');
        }
      }
      );
    }
      // if unable to Search a tweet
      else {
        console.log('Error searching');
      }
    }
  );
}
```

There's a lot going on here. This entire block of code is a single function. We'll take a closer look in a minute, but let's get it working and try it first.

If you tried to run this code right now, it wouldn't actually do anything. You've written a function, but you haven't added any code that will call it. Let's do that now. At the end of this code, add these lines:

```
retweet();
// retweet every 3 minutes
setInterval(retweet, 180000);
```

Now we're calling our function every 180,000 milliseconds, or every 3 minutes. Change this to whatever interval you wish.

> **WARNING** If you run your bot too frequently, Twitter will see that you're using up too many resources and will "rate-limit" you. Once every 3 minutes is plenty.

It's time to try the program. Open your bot's Twitter feed in a web browser. Now in your terminal, run your program by using this command:

```
pi@raspberrypi:~/newtwitbot $ node index.js
```

You'll see lots of output! All the info about each tweet that matches your search string is displayed on your terminal. It is also retweeted to your bot's Twitter account.

Customize Your Own Search

It's not likely that you'll want to keep searching for and retweeting doggo and pupper tweets! You can change the query string (the text in quotes after q:) to look for any terms you wish, including hashtags. Separate multiple terms with commas. The argument result_type: 'recent' tells the code to search for the latest tweets since our bot last retweeted. You can find more parameters for this query string by checking out the Twitter API reference at *dev.twitter.com/rest/reference/get/search/tweets*.

Your program will keep running and retweeting every 3 minutes until you stop it by pressing Ctrl-C.

Let's take a closer look. Consider this code:

```
var params = {
  q: 'watermelon, papaya, mango', result_type: 'recent'
}
```

This code sets up the parameters of the data we'll be searching for.

Here's the code that uses those parameters, starting with the `Twitter.get` function. This function comes from the `twit` API, and it takes three objects:

* The action we want it to take—in this case we want it to search, so we use `search/tweets`.

* The `params` object (our query string and any other params).

* A callback function that calls another `twit` API function, `Twitter.post`. This function does the actual posting or reports errors.

```
Twitter.get('search/tweets', params, function(err, data) {
  // if there no errors
  if (!err) {
    // grab ID of matching tweet
    var retweetId = data.statuses[0].id_str;
    // found something to retweet
    Twitter.post('statuses/retweet/:id',
    {id: retweetId},
      function(err, response) {
        if (response) {
            console.log('Retweeted this tweet');
            console.log(data);
            retweeting.');
        }
    }
    // error while retweeting
    if (err) {
      console.log('Error tweeting';});
    }
    // if unable to search through tweets
    else {
```

```
    console.log('Error searching.');
  }
 });
}
```

The last bit of code we added uses a JavaScript timer function, setInterval(). This timer function calls the retweet function
periodically.

```
retweet();
// retweet every 3 minutes
setInterval(retweet, 180000);
```

We've covered quite a bit of ground in this chapter. Here's the
entire index.js code so far:

```
// Complete index.js code from Chapter 3
// Dependencies
var retweet = function() {
  var params = {
    q: 'doggo OR pupper',
    result_type: 'recent'
  }
  Twitter.get('search/tweets', params, function(err, data) {
    // if there no errors
    if (!err) {
      // grab ID of tweet to retweet
      var retweetId = data.statuses[0].id_str;
      // Tell Twitter to retweet
      Twitter.post('statuses/retweet/:id',
      {
        id: retweetId
      },
      function(err, response) {
        if (response) {
          console.log('Retweeted!!!');
        }
        // if there was an error while tweeting
        if (err) {
          console.log('Error tweeting');
        }
      }
      );
      }
```

```
      // if unable to Search a tweet
      else {
        console.log('Error searching');
      }
    }
  );
}
retweet();
// retweet every 3 minutes
setInterval(retweet, 180000);
```

In the next chapter, we'll expand on the bot's functionality and use the Raspberry Pi to make an LED light up when our bot's Twitter handle is mentioned!

4

Flash an LED in Response to a Twitter Event

You've created your Twitter bot with Node. If you've set it up on your Raspberry Pi, you can hook up an LED and make it flash when an event happens on Twitter.

In this chapter, you'll wire up an LED on a breadboard hooked in to your Pi. Next, you'll write a short program that will make the LED blink twice. Finally, you'll add this code to your Twitter bot program so that each time your bot's Twitter handle is mentioned, the LED will alert you by blinking (Figure 4.1).

FIGURE 4.1: Blinking LED

SET UP THE LED ON YOUR RASPBERRY PI

The setup, shown in Figure 4.2, is fairly simple.
Here's what you'll need:

* Raspberry Pi with 5V power supply

* Breadboard

* 2 male-to-female jumper cables (the example uses black and green)

* An LED

Step 1. Locate the GPIO pins on your Pi (Figure 4.3).

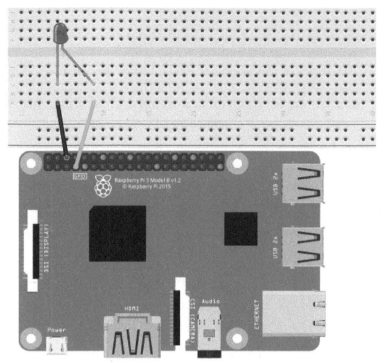

FIGURE 4.2: Complete LED setup on Raspberry Pi

FIGURE 4.3: Close-up of GPIO pins

> ## What Do You Mean by GPIO?
>
> See those 26 pins along one edge of your Pi? Seventeen of these pins are called GPIO, short for General Purpose Input/Output. You can attach external hardware to these pins. The other pins are power or ground pins.

Step 2. Connect the female end of the green jumper cable to pin 4 of the GPIO on the Pi, as shown in both Figures 4.1 and 4.2.

Step 3. Connect the female end of the black jumper cable to pin 3 of the GPIO.

Step 4. Take a look at your LED. One leg is longer than the other. The longer leg is the plus side, and the shorter leg is the minus terminal. This is important to keep track of.

Step 5. Insert your LED into the breadboard as shown in Figure 4.2. Make sure the plus side of the LED is on the right.

Step 6. Connect the male end of the black cable to the breadboard adjacent to the minus terminal of the LED. If any of this is confusing, just take a close look at Figure 4.2.

Step 7. Connect the male end of the green cable to the breadboard adjacent to the plus terminal of the LED.

Your Pi will now be able to blink the LED in response to the code you're about to write!

CREATE THE BLINK PROGRAM

Open your terminal and connect to your Pi. Navigate to the directory where you created your Twitter bot files.

```
pi@raspberrypi:~ $ cd newtwitbot
pi@raspberrypi:~/newtwitbot $
```

Remember using npm to install the Twitter code library called `twit`? We're going to use npm again, this time to import another library called `onoff` that lets us control the LED.

To install this library, use this command:

```
pi@raspberrypi:~/newtwitbot $ npm install --save onoff
```

After `onoff` has finished installing, create and open a new file, `helloBlink.js`.

```
pi@raspberrypi:~/newtwitbot $ nano helloBlink.js
```

This opens the editor with a new blank file. Here's the code to enter:

```
//helloBlink.js
var Gpio = require('onoff').Gpio,
  led = new Gpio(4, 'out');
var iv = setInterval(function () {
  led.writeSync(led.readSync() === 0 ? 1 : 0)
}, 500);
// Toggle state of the LED every half second
setTimeout(function () {
  clearInterval(iv);
  led.writeSync(0);
  // Turn LED off
  led.unexport();
}, 2000);
// End blinking after 2 seconds
```

Save this file.

Now give it a try with the `node` command:

```
pi@raspberrypi:~/newtwitbot $ node helloBlink.js
```

MAKE YOUR BOT DETECT YOUR TWITTER HANDLE

Before your bot can blink in response to your Twitter handle being tweeted, it needs to be able to detect when that happens.

In this section, we'll add some code that will tweet a greeting back to anyone who tweets your handle.

In the last chapter, you created a Twitter bot in a program called index.js. Open index.js (or whatever you named your file) in an editor. We'll add this new code to the end of the current file. Make sure you change *@doggothebotto* to whatever you named your bot!

```
//Respond when someone mentions me, @doggothebotto
var stream = Twitter.stream('statuses/filter',
{ track: ['@doggothebotto'] });
//Look for my @name
stream.on('tweet', tweetEvent);
function tweetEvent(tweet) {
  // Get Twitter handle of who tweeted me
  var name = tweet.user.screen_name;
  // Now send a reply back to the sender
  var reply='You mentioned me! @' + name + ' ' + 'Bork bork!';
  var params = {
    status: reply, in_reply_to_status_id: nameID
  };
  Twitter.post('statuses/update', params,
  function(err, data,response) {
    if (err !== undefined) {
      //Report error if response tweet fails
      console.log(err);
    } else {
      //Report success
      console.log('Tweeted: ' + params.status);
    }
  })
};
```

Basically, this code listens for your bot's Twitter handle. When it detects your handle, it grabs the handle of the sender. Then it creates a reply that includes the sender's handle, and tweets it. In our example, if someone—let's call her @lynnbeighley—were to tweet anything containing my bot's name, @doggothebotto, the bot will respond with You mentioned me! @lynnbeighley Bork bork!.

MAKE YOUR BOT BLINK THE LED WHEN MENTIONED

The last step is to add in the code you used in the `helloBlink.js` program at the correct point in your bot program. You can copy and paste it immediately after this line:

```
console.log('Tweeted: ' + params.status);
```

The complete block of code we added to the end of your bot code in this chapter is

```
//Respond when someone mentions me, @doggothebotto
var stream = Twitter.stream('statuses/filter',
{ track: ['@doggothebotto'] });
//Look for my @name
stream.on('tweet', tweetEvent);
function tweetEvent(tweet) {
  // Get Twitter handle of who tweeted me
  var name = tweet.user.screen_name;
  // Now send a reply back to the sender
  var reply='You mentioned me! @' + name + ' ' + 'Bork bork!';
  var params = {
    status: reply, in_reply_to_status_id: nameID
  };
  Twitter.post('statuses/update', params,
  function(err, data,response) {
    if (err !== undefined) {
      //Report error if response tweet fails
      console.log(err);
    } else {
      //Report success
      console.log('Tweeted: ' + params.status);
var Gpio = require('onoff').Gpio,
  led = new Gpio(4, 'out');
var iv = setInterval(function () {
  led.writeSync(led.readSync() === 0 ? 1 : 0)
}, 500);
// Toggle state of the LED every half second
setTimeout(function () {
  clearInterval(iv);
  led.writeSync(0);
  // Turn LED off
```

```
    led.unexport();
}, 2000);
// End blinking after 2 seconds
    }
  })
};
```

You've now got a bot that not only responds when someone tweets at it, but also blinks an LED to let you know! Using similar techniques, you could monitor Twitter for more practical search terms—for example, the words *tsunami* and *earthquake*.

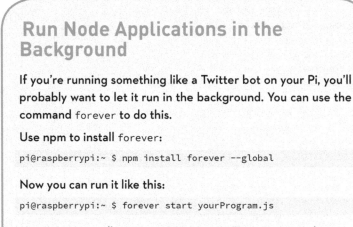

Run Node Applications in the Background

If you're running something like a Twitter bot on your Pi, you'll probably want to let it run in the background. You can use the command forever to do this.

Use npm to install forever:

```
pi@raspberrypi:~ $ npm install forever --global
```

Now you can run it like this:

```
pi@raspberrypi:~ $ forever start yourProgram.js
```

Your program will now run as a process. To stop it, use this:

```
pi@raspberrypi:~ $ forever stop yourProgram.js
```

NODE, PI, AND THE INTERNET OF THINGS

You've now had a jumpstart into JavaScript with Node and Raspberry Pi. You can control real-world devices and interact with the Internet. Blinking an LED is just a small taste of what you can directly control with your Raspberry Pi. Now that you can do that, you can connect and control other, more interesting electronic devices.

For example, you could attach a temperature sensor and periodically post environmental readings to a web page. Or you could use a motion sensor and set up an alert to catch your cat jumping up on your counter at night.

Now it's up to you to dream up and build your own JavaScript/Node/Pi projects!

CPSIA information can be obtained
at www.ICGtesting.com
Printed in the USA
BVHW01s1342060318
509838BV00009B/257/P